# DONKEYS

## Jane Russell

**Grolier**
an imprint of
 SCHOLASTIC
www.scholastic.com/librarypublishing

Published 2009 by Grolier
An Imprint of Scholastic Library Publishing
Old Sherman Turnpike
Danbury, Connecticut 06816

**For The Brown Reference Group plc**
Project Editor: Jolyon Goddard
Picture Researchers: Clare Newman, Sophie
Mortimer
Designer: Sarah Williams
Managing Editor: Tim Harris

Volume ISBN-13: 978-0-7172-8040-7
Volume ISBN-10: 0-7172-8040-3

**Library of Congress
Cataloging-in-Publication Data**

Nature's children. Set 5.
  p. cm.
 Includes index.
 ISBN-13: 978-0-7172-8084-1
 ISBN-10: 0-7172-8084-5 (set)
 1. Animals--Encyclopedias, Juvenile. I.
Grolier Educational (Firm)
 QL49.N386 2009
 590.3--dc22
                        2008014674

Printed and bound in China

**PICTURE CREDITS**

Front Cover: **Shutterstock**: Eimantas Buzas.

Back Cover: **Shutterstock**: Josef Bosak,
Timothy Large, Clarence S. Lewis, Clara
Natoli.

**Alamy**: 42, Chris Howes 33, Tom Kidd 37,
H. Reinhard 26–27; **Corbis**: Steve Kaufman
10; **FLPA**: Tui De Roy 21, Andrew Parkinson
38; **Getty Images**: Purestock 29; **NaturePL**:
Dietmar Nill 30, Pete Oxford 13, Lynn M.
Stone 18; **Photolibrary.com**: 9, 41, 45, 46;
**Shutterstock**: Eimantas Buzas 22, Randy C.
Horne 17, Eric Isselee 4, Jackweichen_gatech
6, Lucwa 5, Rachel Keller Photography 2–3;
**Still Pictures**: Pierre Huguet 14, G. Kopp 34.

# Contents

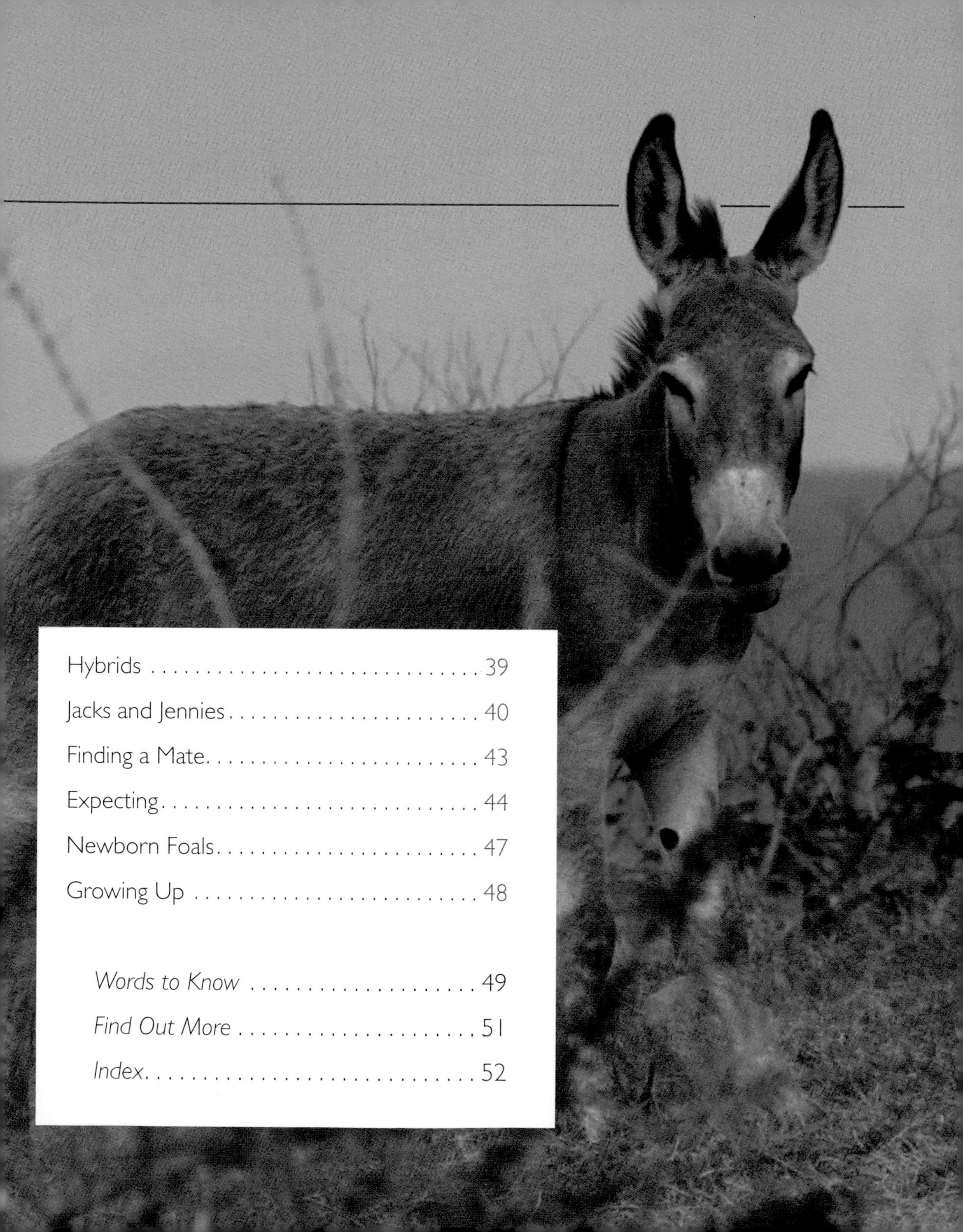

# FACT FILE: Donkeys

| Class | Mammals (Mammalia) |
|---|---|
| Order | Odd-toed hoofed animals (Perissodactyla) |
| Family | Horses, zebras, and asses (Equidae) |
| Genus | *Equus* |
| Species | The donkey is a domestic form of the African wild ass (*Equus asinus*) |
| World distribution | Donkeys are found all over the world; wild asses live in Africa and Asia |
| Habitat | Donkeys are found with humans in all habitats; wild asses live in dry regions |
| Distinctive physical characteristics | A small, sturdy horse with long, upright ears and a tufted tail |
| Habits | Affectionate animals; in the wild, donkeys live in small herds of as many as 10 to 15 animals |
| Diet | Donkeys eat grass, hay, oats, and bran; wild asses eat sparse, dry vegetation |

# Introduction

Donkeys originated in Africa. Thousands of years ago, humans tamed African wild asses to work on farms and carry loads. These tamed asses developed into the donkeys of today.

Donkeys are tough animals. They can survive in harsh, dry places where food and water are difficult to find. Donkeys can work for many hours each day in the hottest places. They also have a gentle side. These long-lived animals often form strong attachments to people, which makes them wonderful companions.

**Donkeys are also known as asses or burros.**

There are between 44 and 60 million donkeys in the world today. About one-fifth of all donkeys, including this one, live in China.

# Part of the Family

Donkeys belong to the horse family, which includes **domestic** horses, the wild Przewalski's (PRIS-VAAL-SKIS) horse, two species of asses, and three species of zebras. All the members of this family have a distinctive "horse" shape. But there are differences, too.

Certain features make it easy to tell apart a donkey and its other domestic relative—the horse. Donkeys are usually smaller than most horses. Donkeys have long, upright ears, an upright mane, and a tufted tail. Horses' ears are smaller, their mane falls to one side, and their tail is long and flowing. Donkeys' **hooves** are smaller and tougher than horses' hooves. Their coat tends to be longer and less oily than a horse's coat, too. Although, like horses, donkeys can be a variety of colors, most donkeys have a brown or gray coat with a dark crosslike marking along their back and across their shoulders.

In addition, donkeys make a "hee-haw" **bray**, or sound, which is different from the "neigh" and "whinny" of horses.

# Ancient Horses

Scientists have found **fossils** of the first horses in North America. These **ancestors** of today's horses were much smaller than modern members of the horse family. The earliest known horse, named *Hyracotherium*, or "eohippus," lived about 50 million years ago. It was about the same size as a red fox—about 1 foot (30 cm) tall at the shoulders. Over millions of years, horses grew bigger. Some of today's domestic horses, for example, can grow as tall as 6 feet (1.8 m) at the shoulders.

Early horses spread across North America. A few million years ago, Alaska was joined to Siberia, in Russia, by a wide "bridge" of land. The horses crossed the bridge into Siberia and spread across Asia and into Africa. Early horses eventually died out in North America, but they survived and developed in other parts of the world. There, they evolved into different species, including zebras, asses, and wild horses.

All members of
the horse family
are fast runners.

The Somali wild ass's legs have black stripes, like those of a zebra.

# African Roots

The African wild ass is the ancestor of donkeys. It once lived all over northern Africa in herds of up to 50 animals. Over a long period of time, the African wild ass developed into two kinds, or subspecies: the Nubian wild ass and the Somali wild ass. The Nubian wild ass has not been seen for many years and is now thought to be **extinct**. The Somali wild ass has survived until now. However, it is struggling and might soon become extinct in the wild.

The Nubian wild ass is the ancestor of all today's donkeys. About 6,000 years ago, it was tamed by farmers in the Nile Valley, in Egypt and Sudan. Domestic asses, or donkeys, became much sought-after animals, and because of their usefulness they gradually spread into other countries. About 2,000 years ago, the Romans brought donkeys from Africa to Europe. And about 500 years ago, European settlers brought donkeys to North America.

# The Asiatic Ass

The Asiatic wild ass lives in an area stretching from northern India to Syria. This ass is very closely related to the donkey. The ancient ancestors of Asiatic and African wild asses became separated and over time **adapted** to different **habitats**.

The Asiatic ass looks and sounds more like a horse than a donkey. It is as big as a horse and nearly as fast as a racehorse. It can run, or gallop, at 40 miles (65 km) per hour and has the endurance to run at that speed for many miles.

Sometimes called the onager (O-NI-JUR), the Asiatic wild ass has never been tamed by humans.

A small herd of
Somali wild asses
grazes together.

14

# Tough Guys

The wild ass had it tough. The zebras and the horses were the big, loud, fast bullies that grabbed most of the land to graze. The ass was pushed out to the edges. The wild ass learned how to find food in the places that were hotter, drier, and higher up. It adapted to these harsh habitats, learning to travel long distances to find water and the sparse, stunted plants that live in such places.

The wild ass has large teeth with flat surfaces for tearing and chewing the toughest kinds of plants. It can last for three days without a drink of water. The wild ass's shaggy coat helps keep the animal warm during cold nights. Its upright ears are good for hearing enemies, and its large nostrils are good for smelling them. Strong, agile legs and narrow upright feet allow it to escape across rough or steep ground. The modern donkey has kept many of these useful features from its wild ancestors.

# Valuable Animals

Historically, donkeys have been honored and valued animals. In ancient times, some people thought so highly of their donkeys that they were buried with them. The Romans sacrificed donkeys—killed donkeys as offerings—to their gods. Cleopatra, a queen of ancient Egypt, was said to take baths in donkey's milk to keep herself beautiful.

In Europe in the **Middle Ages**, the richest and most powerful people particularly prized donkeys. They chose to ride donkeys rather than horses. In the 1500s, the Spanish took donkeys on their ships across the Atlantic Ocean to the Americas. They were used in the exploration of the Americas.

Donkeys' wide-set
eyes allow them
to see almost 360°
around themselves.

17

These donkeys graze on the tough vegetation in the wild country of Nevada.

# All the Same

Burro, ass, and donkey are different names for the same animal. Until the 1500s, donkeys were known as asses. In the English-speaking world, the word *donkey* then took over. No one knows for sure where this word originated from. *Burro* is the Spanish word for donkey.

In the 1500s, Spanish explorers began taking burros across the Atlantic from Spain to what is now Mexico. The burros were then used on long journeys. They carried goods and supplies as travelers explored northward into what is now the United States. Some of these animals escaped into the wild. They survived very well in the dry regions of southern United States. Soon, there were many herds of wild burros. The only difference between them and the domestic donkeys was that they no longer lived with humans. Domestic horses also escaped into the wild. These horses are known as mustangs.

# In the Wild

Domesticated animals that return to the wild are called **feral**. In the 1500s, Spanish burros returned to the wild in the southwestern United States. There were few animals or plants that would kill or poison them. The numbers of feral burros grew quickly.

In areas where there is little food or water, people want to keep what there is for themselves and their own animals. In the United States, too, people soon began to kill the feral burros. They saw the wild burros as competition for food and water. But after a campaign to protect them in 1971, a law was passed making it illegal to hunt and kill burros and mustangs. Today, if numbers of feral burros grow too large there are government roundups, and the donkeys are put up for adoption and taken in by good homes across the country.

These feral donkeys live in the Galápagos Islands. They compete with the islands' giant tortoises for vegetation to graze.

Many donkey owners monitor the weight of their donkeys to make sure that they remain at a healthy weight.

# Donkey Diet

A donkey in the wild can eat tough plants such as thornbush and desert grass. The domestic donkey is not much more demanding. Donkeys have adapted to survive on poor-quality, high-fiber shrubs and grasses. When water is hard to find, donkeys can lose a lot of body fluids—as much as one-third of their body weight—without becoming ill.

Therefore, all that a domestic donkey needs is grass, hay, or barley straw, and a supply of water. Donkeys can also eat a small amount of oats, bran, and corn, and they love vegetable scraps and salt.

Domestic donkeys also appreciate the occasional treats, just like most pets. However, a donkey's digestive system can be overloaded by such food. Without enough exercise they can quickly become overweight.

# Donkey Care

Donkeys have simple needs compared to many other animals. Their diet of grass and hay is available throughout the world. A bed of straw and protection from the sun, rain, and biting insects keep them comfortable. Donkeys do not usually show illness, and it used to be thought that they did not get sick. However, it is now known that donkeys can become very ill before showing any signs of disease.

To keep a donkey healthy, its owner should deworm it regularly. The donkey should also get shots to protect it from the most common donkey diseases, such as distemper, influenza, and tetanus. Some donkeys develop a condition called "sweet itch" from the bites of midges.

A donkey's hooves grow fast. Pet donkeys are usually less active than wild ones, so their hooves need to be trimmed three or four times a year. However, wild donkeys that are always moving around over rough ground wear down their hooves with each step.

# Caretakers

Donkeys are truly special animals. They will look after the young of other animals! If no other donkeys are around, they can form strong emotional bonds with other animals. Horse breeders often keep donkeys as companions for young horses when they are separated from their mother. Donkeys are also used to help train young horses and to act as a soothing influence on very nervous horses.

Donkeys don't like being alone. Pet donkeys like human company. They are especially gentle and protective with young or vulnerable humans. Programs in many parts of the world encourage children and people with disabilities to develop a special bond with a donkey. Donkeys have a good memory, and these friendships can last for a lifetime.

Donkeys are usually calm animals. They do not startle as easily as horses.

# Rides and Trails

In many parts of the world, especially beach resorts, donkeys are used to give rides to children. Some people are concerned about the health and welfare of these donkeys. But in many places, there are now guidelines to ensure the donkeys are treated well and are fit and strong enough to carry children.

Donkeys and **mules**—crosses between horses and donkeys—are used to carry people on various wildlife trails in the United States. Among the most well-known trails is a ride down into the Grand Canyon, in Arizona. The nimble-footed donkeys and mules are suited to the rocky terrain. Some of the trails can take two or three days to complete. The riders travel all the way down to the Colorado River, which flows along the bottom of the canyon.

Donkeys easily
form close bonds
with children.

A donkey pulls a cart of hay for a Bulgarian farmer.

# Beasts of Burden

Despite modern technology, donkeys are still used for many jobs all around the world. In areas where machines are too expensive for local farmers to afford, donkeys are the ideal off-road vehicles. They are often used to pull or carry loads of people or cargo up steep, rocky paths. Donkeys are a lifeline to the outside world for many people living in mountain places.

Donkeys can work in narrow or confined spaces where larger machines or vehicles cannot pass. For example, they can fit between narrow rows of vines or other crops. In Sudan, in Africa, donkeys are used to haul freshwater from the Nile River, over the desert, and down into the towns and cities near the coast. In Mexico, they are used to carry garbage. In a few parts of the world where **droughts** have become common, donkeys are being used more and more as **beasts of burden**. That is because donkeys can withstand the harsh conditions that most other animals cannot.

# Donkeys in Danger

In many parts of the world, donkeys are steadily being replaced by machines. Sadly, that often means that the donkeys are treated badly or abandoned because they are no longer useful. Fortunately, many people want to protect unwanted donkeys. Homes for unwanted donkeys are called **sanctuaries**, and there are many throughout the world.

Peaceful Valley Donkey Rescue is the biggest donkey sanctuary in the United States. Founded in 2000 and located in California, it provides a home for hundreds of abused or neglected donkeys. In addition, the rescue takes in wild burros that are rounded up when their numbers get too high. The Wild Burro Rescue, again in California, also provides food, care, and a safe home for burros.

This new arrival to a donkey sanctuary in Spain is underweight.

Poitou (PWOH-TOO) donkeys are a breed from France. They grow to 15 hands and have a thick, tangled, brown coat.

# Donkey Breeds

Just like dogs, cats, and other domestic animals there are many different **breeds** of donkeys. However, donkeys are usually classified by their coat color and markings, size, or origin—where that type of donkey first came from.

A donkey's height is measured in **hands** from the ground to the withers. The withers are the tops of the shoulders. One hand is equal to 4 inches (10 cm). There are four main donkey sizes. Miniature donkeys, such as the dwarf donkeys of Sicily and India, measure only 6 hands. Standard donkeys grow to 9 to 12 hands. Large standards reach 12 to 14 hands. The tallest donkeys are called mammoth, or jack stock, donkeys. They can reach 16 hands.

# Champions

Certain characteristics, such as strength or unusual coloring, can make some donkeys desirable and valuable. If a donkey is born with unusually good strength it might be used to breed **offspring** that are strong, too. If this characteristic is bred through many generations, a line, or **pedigree**, of strong donkeys will be created.

In some countries, including the United States, donkeys are entered into competitions or shows. Some are judged on how they look, including their coat color, neck length, head size, and how wide-set their eyes are. In the United States, miniature donkeys are often judged on how well they perform being led around an obstacle course.

Donkeys that score well are awarded ribbons or certificates. If a donkey wins many awards it becomes a champion. The offspring of such a donkey have a champion pedigree and are much more valuable than donkeys without any pedigree.

A donkey is given a red ribbon to show it is a winner at a show in Scotland.

A train of mules carries goods across a bridge in Nepal, Asia.

# Hybrids

A cross between two different species is called a **hybrid**. Donkeys can be bred with horses. The offspring of a female horse and a male donkey is called a mule. The offspring of a male horse and a female donkey is called a **hinny**. Hybrids are unusual in the natural world because animals do not normally breed with animals of another species. When hybrids do occur they usually cannot have offspring of their own.

Mules have been bred for hundreds of years. In some places, mules are actually preferred to donkeys. That is because they are often bigger and stronger than either of their parents. Mules behave calmly like donkeys, but are bigger, stronger, and fast like horses.

# Jacks and Jennies

Donkeys, mules, and hinnies are given different names, depending on whether they are male or female. A female donkey is called a jennet or jenny. A male donkey is called a jack or jackass. A female mule or hinny is called a molly, and a male mule or hinny is called a john.

Although most hybrid animals cannot have offspring, female mules very occasionally have babies—and new names are needed! If a female mule breeds with a male donkey the offspring is called a donkule. If the female mule is crossed with a male horse, the offspring is called a hule!

Young donkeys are called **foals**. Female donkey foals are called fillies and male foals are called colts.

A young donkey
is called a foal until
it is one year old.

A male and female donkey will spend time nuzzling and grooming each other.

# Finding a Mate

When it comes to finding a **mate**, wild animals usually look for the strong and reject the weak. Male animals will often fight with one another to prove their strength to females. The future mothers want to be sure the father of their offspring is strong, too.

Donkeys are no exception. Wild jacks fight over jennies. The fighting can cause injuries, so domestic jacks are usually kept away from one another. Farmers and other donkey owners often choose which jacks can mate with which jennies in order to create healthy, strong, and attractive foals.

# Expecting

Female mammals are pregnant for a certain period of time. Offspring born much earlier or later might be weak or might even die. For example, a human pregnancy should be about 38 weeks for a healthy human baby to be born. But jennies can be pregnant from 42 to 57 weeks, depending on their living conditions. If a wild jenny cannot find enough food or water, or is in some other danger, her pregnancy can continue for longer until conditions are more favorable. Even in captivity, the lengths of pregnancies can differ.

Jennies remain very active throughout their pregnancy. They do not even look pregnant until the very end. Then their body finally gets very big and sags with the weight of the foal inside.

This jenny is almost ready to give birth.

A jenny is very protective of her foal.

# Newborn Foals

Jennies make good mothers and often manage to give birth without any help. Once the foal starts to appear, its mother gently helps it out and licks it clean. That helps form a bond between the jenny and her foal. It is important that the newborn foal drinks the very first milk produced by its mother. This early milk contains substances that help prevent or fight disease in the foal.

The size and weight of a newborn foal depend on the size of its parents. On average, foals are 30 to 40 pounds (13.5 to 18 kg) and six hands high. Unlike a human baby, a foal can walk about an hour after being born. The jenny nudges her newborn foal to encourage it onto its feet. Only 24 hours after being born, the foal can move around quickly and confidently. In the wild, that helps it stay away from danger.

# Growing Up

Young donkeys grow faster than young horses. By four months old, they are grazing and no longer need their mother's milk. They eat the same foods as adult donkeys. People who breed donkeys separate the one-year-old jacks from the other donkeys. The jacks with good qualities will be allowed to breed when they are old enough. The other jacks are **neutered** to stop them from fathering any foals of their own.

Foals love to run and play. These activities help the young donkeys grow stronger. Growth continues until a donkey is four years old. By that age, a donkey is strong enough to be ridden and to mate. By four years old, a donkey is also calmer and ready to learn to work.

An average donkey lives to about 27 years. Some donkeys can even live into their forties. That's very long life for a domestic animal. It is certainly not surprising that—even in the age of machines—these gentle but strong creatures are still valued by millions of people across the world.

# Words to Know

**Adapted**    When an animal or plant becomes more suited to the place where it lives and survives more easily.

**Ancestors**    The early types of a living species.

**Beasts of burden**    Animals that are used to carry loads or perform farmwork.

**Bray**    The harsh "hee-haw" sound that a donkey makes.

**Breeds**    Types of domestic donkeys or other domestic animals.

**Domestic**    Bred and tamed by humans.

**Droughts**    Long periods without rain when the land becomes very dry.

**Extinct**    When all of a type of animal is dead and gone forever.

**Feral**    Returned to the wild.

**Foals**    Baby donkeys.

**Fossils**    The preserved remains of ancient plants and animals.

**Habitats**        The types of places where animals and plants live.

**Hands**        Units of horse measurement. One hand is equal to 4 inches (10 cm).

**Hinny**        The offspring of a male horse and a female donkey.

**Hooves**        The hard outer covering on the feet of horses and donkeys.

**Hybrid**        An animal that is a cross between two species.

**Mate**        Either of a breeding pair; to come together to produce young.

**Middle Ages**        The period in history from about 500 to 1500 CE.

**Mules**        The offspring of female horses and male donkeys.

**Neutered**        A medical procedure that prevents an animal from reproducing.

**Offspring**        The young of an animal.

**Pedigree**        The family tree of a certain type of donkey or other animal.

**Sanctuaries**        Safe homes for unwanted animals.

# Find Out More

**Books**

DK Publishing. *Horse*. Eyewitness Books. New York: Dorling Kindersley, 2004.

Wagner, K., and S. Racine. *The Everything Kids' Horses Book: Hours of Off-the-hoof Fun!* Cincinnati, Ohio: Adams Media Corporation, 2006.

**Web sites**

**Donkey**
*www.enchantedlearning.com/subjects/mammals/horse/ Donkeyprintout.shtml*
Facts about donkeys and a printout to color in.

**Wild Horse and Burro Word Search**
*www.fs.fed.us/rangelands/ecology/wildhorseburro/kids/ documents/WHB_Wordsearch.pdf*
A puzzle about donkeys and wild horses.

# Index